bAjC

Listening with Your Eyes

Kids Who Are Deaf and Hard of Hearing

Kids with Special Needs

Seeing with Your Fingers:
Kids with Blindness and Visual Impairment

Listening with Your Eyes:
Kids Who Are Deaf and Hard of Hearing

My Name Is Not Slow:
Kids with Intellectual Disabilities

Sick All the Time: **Kids with Chronic Illness**

Something's Wrong!
Kids with Emotional Disturbance

Speed Racer: **Kids with Attention-Deficit/
Hyperactivity Disorder**

Finding My Voice: **Kids with Speech Impairment**

I Can Do It! **Kids with Physical Challenges**

The Hidden Child: **Kids with Autism**

What's Wrong with My Brain?
Kids with Brain Injury

Why Can't I Learn Like Everyone Else?
Kids with Learning Disabilities

Listening with Your Eyes
Kids Who Are Deaf and Hard of Hearing

by Sheila Stewart and Camden Flath

MASON CREST PUBLISHERS INC.
370 Reed Road
Broomall, Pennsylvania 19008
(866)MCP-BOOK (toll free)
www.masoncrest.com

First Printing
9 8 7 6 5 4 3 2 1

ISBN (set) 978-1-4222-1727-6   ISBN (pbk set) 978-1-4222-1918-8

Library of Congress Cataloging-in-Publication Data

Stewart, Sheila, 1975–
  Listening with your eyes : kids who are deaf and hard of hearing / by Sheila Stewart and Camden Flath.
      p. cm.
  ISBN 978-1-4222-1717-7   ISBN (pbk) 978-1-4222-1920-1
  1. Deaf children—Juvenile literature. 2. Deafness in children—Juvenile literature. 3. Hearing impaired children—Juvenile literature. I. Flath, Camden, 1987– II. Title.
  HV2392.S74 2010
  362.4'2083—dc22
                              2010004979

Produced by Harding House Publishing Service, Inc.
www.hardinghousepages.com
Design by MK Bassett-Harvey.
Cover design by Torque Advertising Design.
Printed in the USA by Bang Printing.

Photo Credits
Creative Commons Attribution 2.0 Generic/Unported: Camazine: pg. 34, mricon: pg. 37; GNU Free Documentation License, Version 1.2; morgueFile: jdurham: pg. 38, taliesin: pg. 31; United States Air Force; United States Army; Ford, Kyle: pg. 40

The creators of this book have made every effort to provide accurate information, but it should not be used as a substitute for the help and services of trained professionals.

Introduction

To the Teacher

Kids with Special Needs provides a unique forum for demystifying a wide variety of childhood medical and developmental disabilities. Written to captivate an elementary-level audience, the books bring to life the challenges and triumphs experienced by children with common chronic conditions such as hearing loss, intellectual disability, physical differences, and speech difficulties. The topics are addressed frankly through a blend of fiction and fact.

This series is particularly important today as the number of children with special needs is on the rise. Over the last two decades, advances in pediatric medical techniques have allowed children who have chronic illnesses and disabilities to live longer, more functional lives. At the same time, IDEA, a federal law, guarantees their rights to equal educational opportunities. As a result, these children represent an increasingly visible part of North American population in all aspects of daily life. Students are exposed to peers with special needs in their classrooms, through extracurricular activities, and in the community. Often, young people have misperceptions and unanswered questions about a child's disabilities—and more important, his or her abilities. Many times, there is no vehicle for talking about these complex issues in a comfortable manner.

This series will encourage further conversation about these issues. Most important, the series promotes a greater comfort for its readers as they live, play, and study side by side with these children who have medical and developmental differences—kids with special needs.

—Dr. Carolyn Bridgemohan
Boston Pediatric Hospital/Harvard Medical School

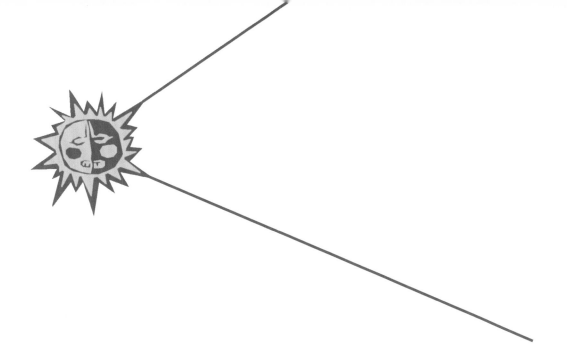

Abby stared out of the window of the school bus, watching the rain fall. Trees, houses, and people went by outside.

Inside the bus, even without looking at them, Abby could tell the other kids were excited about the first day of school. From the corner of her eye, she could see kids bouncing in their seats, and every once in a while someone hit the back of her seat. She knew they must be loud, because when she looked she could see the bus driver's mouth opening wide, like he was yelling.

She wondered what her teacher would be like this year. Ms. Doyle was new so no one knew anything about her. Sometimes teachers acted annoyed that she had a sign language interpreter or that she needed copies of the class notes or even sometimes just that she couldn't hear. Fifth grade was an important year; a bad teacher could ruin everything.

The bus stopped and the kids got louder. She could see their noise in their energy. She felt like she could almost feel the noise prickling on her skin. But she couldn't hear anything. If she closed her eyes, she might as well have been alone.

Brennan, her interpreter, was waiting for her in the classroom at a table near the teacher's desk, although it was off to one side so his interpreting didn't distract the other kids. She kind of had a crush on Brennan, but he and his wife had just had a baby girl, so she supposed she couldn't marry him after all.

"Hey Abby!" Brennan said, speaking the words with his lips and signing at the same time. "How was your summer? How was camp?"

"Great!" she signed.

Every summer she spent a week at a camp for kids who were deaf and hard of hearing. She loved getting to be at place where she was just like everyone else for a change. She started to tell Brennan more about it, but he stopped her.

"Say the words while you sign."

She didn't like talking in class, because she could never tell how loud her voice was, but she started again, telling Brennan about her summer.

The class had mostly filled up while she was talking to Brennan. A woman was standing behind the teacher's desk, looking at a laptop. The woman was not old, but not really young, either. She wore a blue flowered dress and had bright red hair. She turned around and wrote "Ms. Doyle" on the white board in big curly letters.

Ms. Doyle turned out to be a pretty good teacher. She kept her head turned toward Abby when she talked, so that Abby could work on lip reading. Abby wasn't always very good at lip reading, but her parents and her speech therapist kept telling her to practice more.

Ms. Doyle also gave Abby handouts of the class notes at the end of each day. She never seemed bothered by doing this, and she didn't seem to mind Brennan either, so she immediately became Abby's favorite teacher ever.

Mostly, nobody in class tried to talk to Abby. Sometimes people smiled at her. If they did have to say something, they usually talked with big, exaggerated lip movements that were impossible to understand.

During the third week of school, Abby looked up during lunch and saw the girl—she thought her name was Madison—say the word "party."

Sometimes, Abby practiced lip reading in the cafeteria, so she kept watching. "We'll invite everyone!" another girl—Victoria?—said.

"Well, not *everyone*," Madison said, and suddenly all the girls turned and looked straight at Abby.

At supper that night, Abby didn't feel like eating. Her mom had made lasagna, which was her favorite, but she wasn't hungry.

All around the table, her family talked and laughed. They used their hands when they talked, so she wouldn't be left out. Her parents had always insisted on that, even though Abby was the only one who couldn't hear.

"We're a family," her father had told her. "We love each other, and no one is going to be left out."

Sometimes Abby felt left out anyway, but she did love her family. Her brother Max was a senior in high school and just about the coolest person she knew. Her older sisters, Julie and Lauren, were amazing and gorgeous. Especially Julie, who was fifteen and sometimes helped Abby style her hair and put on makeup. Her little brother, Tyler, was seven and a pest, but he was still a good kid.

Tyler was the one who first noticed something was wrong with Abby. "Why aren't you eating?" he asked, talking with his mouth full and signing at the same time. "Are you okay?"

Everybody stopped eating and looked at Abby.

"Do you feel all right?" Her looked worried.

"Just not hungry," Abby signed, refusing to look them in the eyes.

Lauren grabbed Abby's face and made her look at her. "Nope," she said. "Something happened. You're really sad."

Eventually, Abby's family coaxed the whole story out of her. She was used to being ignored and left out at school, but not being invited to a party still hurt. Her brothers and sisters were her best friends, but she wished she could have friends at school too, like other kids did.

Julie and Lauren hugged her after she'd told them about it.

"Do you want me to beat up Madison for you?" Max flexed his muscles and put on a scary face. The thought of Max hurting anyone, let alone a fifth-grade girl, was so unbelievable that Abby laughed.

Laughing made her feel a little better, but she was still upset. "Why does everyone at school hate me?" she asked.

"They don't hate you, sweetheart," her mom said. "They just don't know how to talk to people who are different from themselves."

"That doesn't help me any," Abby said. "I just wish I was like everyone else."

"I know you do," her dad said. "But we love you just the way you are. One day you will find friends who feel the same way."

"When?" Abby's best friend, Liz, had moved away two years ago, and her other friends had drifted away after that. Liz had been the glue that held them and Abby together.

"I don't know when," her dad said, "but it *will* happen. Why don't you try to talk to the other kids? Tell them how you feel?"

But Abby didn't think she could do that.

The next day, Abby kept noticing kids talking about the party. Apparently, there was going to be games and dancing and food. Madison and Victoria and a couple of their friends were secretly working on invitations instead of doing math. Abby wasn't sure why they even needed invitations when everyone knew they were invited. Maybe just to make it more obvious that she wasn't invited.

Ms. Doyle knew Madison wasn't doing her work. Abby was watching her teacher, and she could see the moment when Ms. Doyle decided that she had better tell Madison to put the invitations away and do her work.

"What's this?" Ms. Doyle asked Madison, while Abby read her lips.

Madison had her back to Abby, but Abby figured she was telling Ms. Doyle about the party. She was waving her hands and point to the invitations on her desk.

"So this is the list of everyone who's invited?" Ms. Doyle asked, and Madison nodded.

Ms. Doyle picked up the piece of paper and looked at it. "The whole class is on here except for Abby."

Madison shrugged and squirmed. She turned her head to look at Abby, and Abby read what part of what she was saying. ". . . she's deaf, Ms. Doyle. She wouldn't care about the party anyway."

Abby thought she was going to cry. She wanted to run out of the room. Maybe she'd run all the way over to the high school and get Max to come beat up Madison after all. She turned her chair so she was facing the wall and refused to look at anyone. Brennan tried to talk to her, but she ignored him and wouldn't look at him either.

When the school day was over, she tried to leave quickly, without meeting anyone's eyes, but Ms. Doyle touched her shoulder.

"I need to talk to you," she said, when Abby looked up. "Your mom is coming to pick you up, so you don't need to worry about the bus."

She waited until the other kids had left the room, and then she motioned Abby to sit down. Brennan perched on the edge of a table in case he was needed.

"I know you saw what Madison said earlier," Ms. Doyle said. "The other students don't understand what it's like to be deaf. With your permission, I'd like to talk to them about it, and maybe do an activity that will help them understand what it's like not to be able to hear."

Abby didn't want to be there when Ms. Doyle talked to the class about deafness. She thought the idea was okay, she just didn't want to be around. She couldn't stand to see everyone staring at her while Ms. Doyle talked about her. Her mom and Ms. Doyle finally agreed to let her stay home the next day, although Ms. Doyle gave her a pile of homework to keep her busy.

Abby didn't know what to expect when she walked into class the day after Ms. Doyle's experiment. She told herself that everything would be the same as it had always been. She couldn't really imagine it being any different.

Instead, Victoria came to meet her, looking nervous. "Hi, Abby." She spoke normally, instead of over-exaggerating her words, so Abby could read her lips.

"Hi." Abby hoped she was talking at the right volume.

"Yesterday was really interesting." Victoria still looked nervous. "Ms. Doyle had us take turns wearing earplugs and big headphones. You could hardly hear anything with them on. It was weird. And people just stopped talking to you while you were wearing them,

since you wouldn't hear them anyway." She looked at Abby to see if she was understanding her.

Abby nodded, and Victoria went on. "Anyway, I just wanted to say I'm sorry for ignoring you. And Madison and I want to invite you to the party on Saturday. Please come."

At first, Abby wasn't sure if she wanted to go to the party. What if she went and then everyone ignored her anyway? Or worse, made fun of her?

"Of course you should go!" Lauren told her that evening, and Julia offered to help her get ready.

When Madison handed her an invitation the next day at school, Abby found herself agreeing to go. So she was going to a party. She still didn't know whether she was more excited or nervous, though.

A lot more people at school were saying hi to her and treating her like she was actually there. Victoria had started talking to her every day and sitting with her at lunch. She liked Victoria, but she was afraid

Victoria didn't really want to be her friend, that she just felt guilty about being mean and ignoring her.

On Saturday evening, her mom dropped her off at Madison's house for the party. "I'll be back at nine," her mom told her, "but you can text me if you need me to come earlier."

Abby nodded. She had Max's cell phone in her pocket, set on vibrate so she could tell if it rang. She took a deep breath and walked up the path to Madison's front door.

When the door opened, light and movement and vibrations washed over Abby. She blinked and stepped inside. Madison was holding the door, and kids were dancing in the room behind her. Madison said something to Abby, but she seemed to be shouting and Abby couldn't read her lips. She pointed to another room, and Abby followed her into a kitchen. Snacks and pizza were set out on the table, and kids hung around eating and talking. Victoria saw her and came over.

"Hey Abby!" Then she said something else Abby couldn't understand.

"Speak normally," Abby told Victoria.

"What?" Victoria asked.

It must really be loud in here, Abby thought. She saw a white board on the fridge and pulled Victoria over to it.

"I can't read your lips when you shout," she wrote.

"And I can't hear you because it's so noisy!" Victoria wrote. They looked at each other and laughed.

"Do you want something to eat?" Victoria asked, speaking more naturally.

"I kind of want to dance first," Abby wrote.

"Really? But you can't hear the music. . . ." Victoria looked confused.

"I'll show you," Abby wrote.

They went into the living room, and Abby found a speaker. She put her hand against it and felt the pulse of the music against her hand. She started dancing to

the beat. She'd danced with her brothers and sisters lots of times; it was one of their favorite things to do together.

Beside her, Victoria started to dance too. Moving in time to the music's rhythm, the two girls smiled at each other.

Kids and Deafness

Kids who are deaf can't hear sounds; kids who are hard of hearing hear differently than children without hearing loss. Some kids may be hard of hearing and have trouble understanding everything that is said to them. They may miss an important direction in a long list because of a nearby sound. Children who are considered deaf may not be able to hear much speech and need to use other forms of communication.

Each person's hearing loss is different. Hearing loss doesn't only affect the amount of sound a person can hear; the way people with hearing loss experience sound is also different from person to person. Some people may

Some types of hearing loss make it more difficult to hear one sound when there are many sounds at once.

not be able to hear quiet sounds, while others may hear all sounds as very quiet. For some kids with hearing loss, sounds may get muddled together or be hard to understand.

Kids who have hearing loss aren't different in any way except their ability to hear. They can do well in the classroom, on the playground, and at home. Kids who have hearing loss can be great friends, teammates, and students. They deserve the same respect and understanding that everyone does.

How Do We Hear?

Sound is a form of energy. This energy travels in waves. Sound waves are created when *molecules* move back

Molecules are the tiniest pieces of something.

and forth very quickly. This is called vibration. When you drop a basketball on the ground, for example, the molecules of the ball and the ground hit against

All sound waves are caused by molecules vibrating.

each other and vibrate, causing sound waves. We hear something when those waves of sound reach our ears.

Many parts of the ear work together to make hearing possible. The ear has three main parts: the outer ear (the part you can see), the middle ear, and the inner ear. Each of these parts have parts of their own. The outer ear collects sound waves (like a funnel) and sends them down the ear canal, a tube that takes sound to the middle ear.

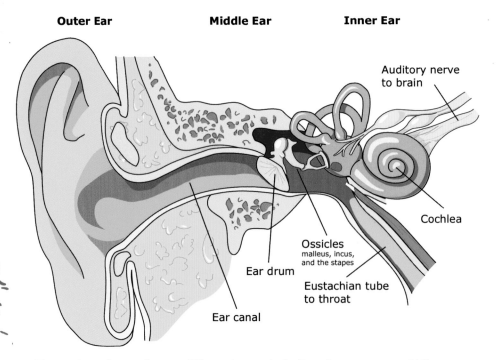

Outer Ear   **Middle Ear**   **Inner Ear**

Auditory nerve
to brain

Cochlea

Ossicles
malleus, incus,
and the stapes

Ear drum

Eustachian tube
to throat

Ear canal

The ear is made up of many different parts, including the outer ear, middle ear, and inner ear.

When the sound waves reach the middle ear, they hit the eardrum. The eardrum is made of very thin material. When sound hits that material, it vibrates (just like the head of a drum does when you hit it with a stick). The vibrations in the eardrum makes three very tiny bones behind the eardrum—called the malleus, the incus, and the stapes— to also vibrate. As sound energy travels from the outer ear down the ear canal to the middle ear, the vibrations become weaker, the vibrating of the bones behind the eardrum **amplifies** the sound waves so they can travel to the inner ear.

Sound waves coming into the inner ear enter the co-chlea, a part of the ear that looks a little like a snail. Inside the cochlea, vibrations move

Amplifies *means to make something louder or stronger.*

through a liquid and make thousands of tiny hair cells vibrate as well. The hair cells trigger the nerves that send a message to the brain. We understand that message as "sound."

What Causes Hearing Loss?

With so many different parts of the ear and brain having to work together, there are many things that can cause hearing loss. In general, there are two types of hearing loss: genetic and nongenetic hearing loss.

Genetic hearing loss is passed down from parents to their children. If one or both parents have a *gene* for hearing loss, they can pass it to their child. If neither parent has a gene for hearing loss, they can still have a child with altered hearing, but this would be caused by gene *mutation*. Chemicals, illnesses, or pollution can cause

A gene carries the information by which parents pass along traits (such as eye color, intelligence, height) to their children.

A mutation is when a gene is damaged so that the message it carries is changed.

gene mutation. Around 30 percent of kids who are deaf or hard of hearing have genetic hearing loss. That means if you had a group of 100 children who were deaf or hard

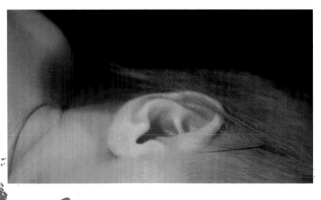

A baby can be born with hearing loss or develop hearing loss later in life.

of hearing, about 30 of them would have hearing loss caused by genetics.

Nongenetic hearing loss means that the child's genes are not the cause of hearing loss. Instead, some other outside factor causes loss of hearing. This may happen before the baby is born, if the mother is **exposed** to dangerous chemicals or gets very sick. Babies who are born with normal hearing can also become deaf or hard of hearing later in life. Sicknesses like *meningitis*, chicken pox, and mumps can cause hearing loss, for example. If a child is exposed to a very loud sound, or loud sound for a long period of time, she can also develop a hearing loss. A head injury can hurt the ear and cause hearing loss, as well.

Exposed means that someone was put in a place where she was laid open to danger or harm.

Meningitis is a serious infection of the brain or spinal cord.

The auditory system is all the parts of your body that help you hear.

Other nongenetic causes of hearing loss include:

- *Medicines:* Certain medicines can damage the ***auditory system***, causing some form hearing loss.
- *Lack of oxygen:* If a baby doesn't get enough oxygen before she is born, she may be born with some hearing loss.

- **_Premature_** _birth:_ If a baby is born prematurely, before his hearing is fully-developed, he may be born with hearing loss.

Levels of Hearing Loss

Kids who are deaf or hard of hearing may have different levels of hearing. The amount of hearing a child who is deaf or hard of hearing has left is called residual hearing. A child with a lot of residual hearing would be diagnosed as hard of hearing. If a child has very little or no residual hearing, they would be diagnosed as deaf. Very few deaf people can hear no sound at all.

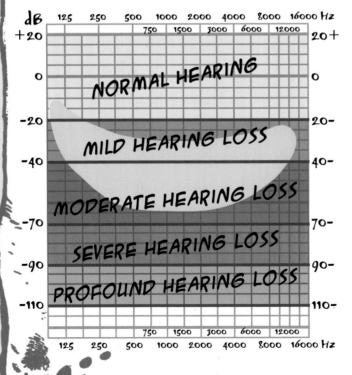

Each level of hearing loss describes the amount of sound that a person with hearing loss can still hear, called residual hearing.

Hearing loss is ranked into four levels, based on the amount of sound a person can hear:

- **Mild** *hearing loss:* A person with mild hearing loss is able to hear voices, but she can understand only some of what is said. She may also have a hard time hearing people speak who are far away or while there are other noises around. This means that a child with mild hearing loss might understand only some of what she is being told in a classroom or by a parent.

- **Moderate** *hearing loss:* Moderate hearing loss might cause a person to miss most of what someone is saying to him. He may be able to hear better if the person talking to him is very close to him. He may also be able to use the speaker's expressions and lip movements to understand what is being said. He will have a harder time hearing the further away the speaker is and the harder it is for him to see the speaker's face.

- **Severe** *hearing loss:* If someone has severe hearing loss, she will have trouble hearing most of the time.

> *Premature means that something happened sooner or earlier than it should have.*
>
> *Mild means not serious, not very bad.*
>
> *Moderate means medium, average.*
>
> *Severe means serious, very bad.*

A child with severe hearing loss may not understand speech unless it is very loud and very close. Severe hearing loss may mean that a person cannot understand any speech at all unless she is lip reading.

- *Profound hearing loss:* A person with profound hearing loss will need help from sign language or lip reading to understand speech.

How Is Deafness Diagnosed?

Sometimes a child may go many years without anyone knowing he has some form of hearing loss. Teachers may think he is struggling with class work because he has a learning difficulty, not realizing that he isn't hearing much of what goes on in the classroom. Parents may think he is daydreaming all the time and not paying attention, when really he just can't hear. The child himself doesn't realize that everyone doesn't hear the way he does. He may learn to make up for his loss of hearing by using expressions or lip reading to understand what people are saying.

Profound means complete, total.

Tests for hearing loss are done by an audiologist, an expert in hearing and hearing loss. The audiologist first tests for how much sound a child can hear. This is mea-

An audiologist uses a machine like this to help her diagnose hearing problems.

sured in decibels. By measuring how much sound a child is hearing, the audiologist can learn which level of hearing loss (from mild to profound) a child has.

Once the level of hearing loss is known, the audiologist begins to look for where the hearing loss is happening. There may be problems with the outer or middle ear, a problem with the cochlea, or a problem with the brain understanding sound information. An audiologist will also check to see if a child has the same amount of hearing in each ear, and whether or not she is continuing to lose hearing.

Deafness and Communication

If a child has difficulty hearing speech, he may have trouble learning language. If someone cannot hear speech at all, he will likely have trouble speaking himself. Children

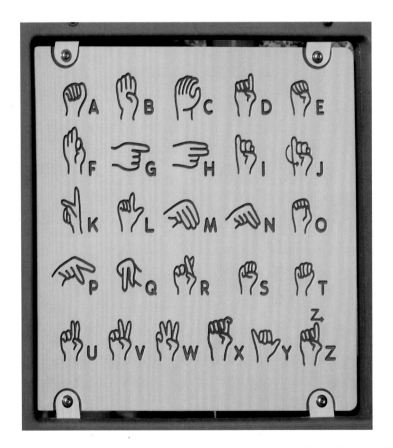

Sign language is a language of hand gestures that allows people with hearing loss to communicate with others without speaking or making sound.

who are deaf or hard of hearing have different options when it comes to finding ways to communicate. Many kids who are deaf or hard of hearing can learn to speak and lip read. Many will also learn to use sign language.

Sign Language

Sign language uses hand movements and gestures to express language. In the United States, kids who are deaf or hard of hearing can use American Sign Language (ASL) to speak to others using their hands. Countries around the world have their own forms of sign language. ASL isn't just English translated into hand signals, it's another language all its own.

Hearing Aid

A hearing aid is a small device that fits inside the ear. It amplifies all sound entering the ear, allowing some people with hearing loss to hear better. Hearing aids aren't for everyone, though. They may help

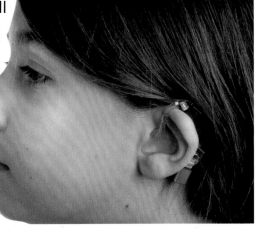

A hearing aid fits snuggly in the ear of someone with hearing loss.

Hearing aids make sounds louder, but not clearer.

make sounds louder, but hearing aids do not improve everything about a person's hearing. An FM system can be used to make hearing aids work better by using a microphone that sends the sound directly to a receiver in the hearing aid.

Cochlear Implant

A cochlear implant is another tool used to improve hearing. If the cochlea is damaged inside the ear, sound waves cannot be turned into signals to be sent to the brain. A cochlear implant uses a microphone outside a person's head to amplify sound. This sound is then sent to a device inside the head that turns the sound into the signals the brain can understand as sound. Cochlear implants aren't for all kinds of hearing loss, but they can help some people hear much better.

School and Deafness

Many kids who are deaf or hard of hearing will sit in class with children who don't have any hearing loss. Others may need some help learning language. A language *specialist* can help kids who have difficulty hearing keep up with kids who don't have hearing loss. Kids with hearing loss should also sit close to the front of the class so that they can read the lips of the teacher better. A note-taker and *interpreter* who knows sign language can help kids with hearing loss in the classroom, as well.

Not all kids who are deaf or hard of hearing will need *special education*. For some, however, it will be the best way for them to learn and suc-ceed in school. Many kids with hearing loss will have no trou-ble in a classroom with kids without hearing loss. Kids with profound hearing loss will likely need special help in school.

A law called the Individuals with Disabilities Education Act (IDEA) outlines how schools should decide which kids need special education. In order to *qualify* for special education under IDEA, the child's hear-ing loss must get in the way of his learning or taking part in school activities.

A *specialist* is a person who has learned to do one particular skill or job.

An *interpreter* is someone who translates one language into another.

Special education teaches kids who have trouble learning because of some disability.

To *qualify* means to fit the definition of something or to meet the requirements.

The IDEA law lists thirteen different kinds of *disabilities* that may mean a child will qualify for special education. Deafness and hearing *impairment* are two different categories under the law.

The IDEA law requires that:

- the child has problems performing well at school activities.
- the child's parent, teacher, or other school staff person must ask that the child be examined for a disability.
- the child is *evaluated* to decide if she does indeed have a disability and to figure out what kind of special education she needs.
- a group of people, including the kid's parents, teachers, and a hearing specialist, meets to decide on a plan for helping him (or her). This plan is called an Individualized Education Program (IEP). The IEP spells out exactly what the child needs in order to succeed at school.

Disabilities are problems—either physical or mental—that get in the way of a person doing what other people can do.

An *impairment* is an injury or something that keeps a person from being able to do the things other people can.

When something is *evaluated*, it is examined to see in which category it belongs.

Understanding Deafness

Kids who are deaf or hard of hearing will face challenges. Kids with hearing loss may feel like they don't fit in with others. Being with other people who are deaf or hard of hearing may help them feel better. There is an entire community of people who are deaf who support each other.

*To **vocalize** means to speak out loud.*

Different families may choose to help handle deafness in different ways. Some children may speak only sign language. Others may **vocalize** and lip read. Still others may

Many people who are deaf or hard of hearing may communicate using sign language. They may also read lips and vocally communicate when possible.

do both. Some may choose to wear a hearing aid or have a cochlear implant, while others will not. Whatever they choose, kids with hearing loss should always be treated with respect.

Today, most children with hearing loss are able to take part in the same activities as other kids. Children who are deaf or hard of hearing can be just as successful at school, on the playground, and at home as kids who have no hearing loss.

Hearing loss is just one part of whom someone is. A kid who is deaf or hard of hearing will also have things she likes and doesn't like, just like anyone else. She will be good at some things and not so good at others. She can be funny or serious, shy or outgoing, artistic or good at math. Once you get to know her, you'll find she's more like you than she is different!

To allow people who are deaf or hard of hearing to enjoy a speech, sermon, or other public speaking event, an interpreter may translate what the speaker is saying into sign language.

Further Reading

Anderson, J. *My Hearing Loss and Me: We Get Along Most of the Time.* Bloomington, Ind.: Trafford Publishing, 2004.

Basinger, C. *Everything You Need to Know About Deafness.* New York: Rosen Publishing Group, 2000.

Kent, D. *American Sign Language.* London: Franklin Watts, 2003.

Kramer, J. *You Can Learn Sign Language!* New York: Scholastic, 2004.

Landau, E. *The Sense of Hearing.* New York: Scholastic, 2009.

Levete, S. *Explaining Deafness.* Mankato, Minn.: Smart Apple Media, 2009.

Martin, M. *Deaf Child Crossing.* New York: Aladdin Paperbacks, 2004.

Schneider, E. E. *Taking Hearing Impairment to School.* New York: JayJo Books, 2004.

Silverstein, A. *Hearing.* Brookfield, Conn.: Twenty-First Century Books, 2001.

Find Out More On the Internet

Alexander Graham Bell Association for the Deaf and Hard of Hearing
www.agbell.org

American Speech-Language-Hearing Association
www.asha.org

Clarke School for the Deaf/Center for Oral Education
www.clarkeschool.org

Deaf.com
www.deaf.com

DeafAndHH.com
www.deafandhh.com

National Association of the Deaf
www.nad.org

The National Dissemination Center for Children with Disabilities
(NICHCY)
www.nichcy.org

National Institute on Deafness and Other Communications
Disorders
www.nidcd.nih.gov

Rochester School For the Deaf
www.rsdeaf.org

Disclaimer

The websites listed on this page were active at the time of publication. The publisher is not responsible for websites that have changed their address or discontinued operation since the date of publication. The publisher will review and update the websites upon each reprint.

Index

About the Authors

Sheila Stewart has written several dozen books for young people, both fiction and nonfiction, although she especially enjoys writing fiction. She has a master's degree in English and now works as a writer and editor. She lives with her two children in a house overflowing with books, in the Southern Tier of New York State.

Camden Flath is a writer living and working in Binghamton, New York. He has a degree in English and has written several books for young people. He is interested in current political, social, and economic issues and applies those interests to his writing.

About the Consultant

Dr. Carolyn Bridgemohan is board certified in developmental behavioral pediatrics and practices at the Developmental Medicine Center at Children's Hospital Boston. She is the director of the Autism Care Program and an assistant professor at Harvard Medical School. Her specialty areas are autism and other pervasive developmental disorders, developmental and learning problems, and developmental and behavioral pediatrics.

NA